This book belongs to:

____

Made in the USA
Columbia, SC
17 December 2019

85196391R00061